Original title:
Life: Just Trying to Keep It Together

Copyright © 2025 Creative Arts Management OÜ
All rights reserved.

Author: Eleanor Prescott
ISBN HARDBACK: 978-1-80566-121-4
ISBN PAPERBACK: 978-1-80566-416-1

## **Mosaic of Moments**

Juggling socks and missing keys,
Spilling coffee, oh what a breeze!
Laughing loud at all my slips,
Life's a movie, with a few skips.

Balancing acts on wobbly chairs,
Sliding into chaos, no time for prayers.
Chasing dreams that tend to scatter,
Finding joy in all the clatter.

## **Threads of Resilience**

Stitching this quilt of yesterday's tears,
Each patch a tale from all those years.
Laughter in seams, a cheeky smile,
Worn and frayed, but full of style.

Tangled hair and mismatched socks,
Dodging life's unexpected knocks.
With a wink to fate, I roll my eyes,
Sowed with humor and sweet surprise.

**Navigating the Stormy Seas**

Sailing boats with holes below,
Paddling hard, but oh so slow!
Waves of chaos crash and fall,
Yet here I stand, I'll brave it all.

Anchor's lost, and sails are torn,
Still I laugh, though slightly worn.
Navigating storms with goofy glee,
Who knew disaster could be so free?

## **Unraveled but Unyielding**

Threads unspooled, a colorful mess,
But oh, what fun in such distress!
Knots entwined like a wild dance,
I'll weather woes with a silly glance.

Slippers mismatched, shoes untied,
Through ups and downs, I'll take it in stride.
With a chuckle and a glance askew,
I'll thread this needle, just watch me do!

## **Unraveled but Unbroken**

My socks mismatch, shoes untied,
Coffee spills, I slide and glide.
The cat's on the ceiling, what a sight,
Perhaps it's time for a nap tonight.

Juggling cereal, oh what a feat,
While dodging the dog who thinks I'm a treat.
The plants are thirsty, the dishes stack high,
If chaos is art, then I'm a supply!

The world's a circus, I'm the clown,
Twirling and whirling, oh I won't drown!
My to-do list is a scroll on the floor,
Yet somehow, I'm still wanting more!

With laughter as glue, I'll craft my way,
Through sticky messes that greet every day.
Unraveled, sure, but my spirit's in flight,
Keep on laughing, it'll be all right!

## Dancing on the Edge of Instability

Balancing books atop my head,
While wondering if I've been misled.
A dinner date with spaghetti, oh dear,
Flying noodles in chaotic cheer!

Tap dancing on the fridge at night,
With yogurt cups as my spotlight.
The neighbors watch, but I don't care,
I'll boogie like I'm dancing on air!

My phone's on silent, where did it go?
Oh, there it is, in the ice cream dough!
Trying to focus on a TV show,
But a squirrel just stole my brilliant glow.

In a whirl of fun, I find my ground,
In the chaos, joy is what I've found.
Each stumble's a dance, a step in the game,
Dancing on edges, but who's to blame?

## A Tapestry of Unfinished Stories

I've started a novel, chapter one,
But my cat's the main character—oh what fun!
With paw prints scattered on every page,
A feline epic, why not engage?

Scribbles in notebooks, thoughts run wild,
A plot twist inspired by a coffee-stained child.
The toaster's a villain, the forks are the crew,
Plot thickens nicely, as drama ensues!

A sock puppet named Steve argues with me,
About the merits of sandwich vs. tea.
"Choose wisely," he says, with a wink and a grin,
A tapestry woven from laughter within.

So here's to the tales that never quite finish,
To stories we start, but don't quite diminish.
In this grand saga of twists and tangles,
In unfinished chapters, joyous life dangles!

## Beneath the Surface of the Storm

Rain threatens to ruin my hair,
But I've got an umbrella—oh, what a flare!
Clouds gather like unscheduled guests,
Yet I'm dancing around, feeling quite blessed.

Puddles form like mirrors of fate,
Both deep and shallow, they can wait.
Winds may howl with tales of dread,
But I wear my socks—who cares if they're red?

**Chasing Shadows and Sunlight**

I run, I trip, to catch that sun,
But shadows just laugh, 'This isn't fun!'
They stretch and tease as I leap about,
Chasing warm rays, filled with doubt.

A game of tag under the sky,
With laughter echoing, oh my, oh my!
The sun peeks out, then hides away,
While I juggle my tasks, come what may.

## The Weight of Unspoken Words


A heavy heart in a light balloon,
Words float away, like a lost tune.
I practice my speech in the shower's steam,
But the audience? A rubber duck's dream!

In conversations with socks on the floor,
I spill my thoughts—wait, there's more!
They listen hard with their fabric ears,
While I pack my hopes in forgotten cheers.

## A Canvas of Scattered Thoughts

Doodles of worries across my mind,
A mix of colors—oh, how I'm confined!
Brush strokes of chaos in every hue,
It seems my planner's turned into a zoo!

Post-its flutter like butterflies lost,
Reminding me daily of the lines crossed.
Yet I smile at the chaos, it's part of the art,
In this wild gallery—I've found my heart.

## Silhouettes of Resilience

My socks never match, what a sight,
Coffee spills give me quite a fright.
Yet, I stand firm in my messy domain,
Wishing for sunshine, not this rain.

The cat's on my keyboard, typing away,
While I ponder what's for dinner today.
Lost my keys but found a shoe,
In this circus of life, I'm the star, it's true!

Emails piling up, a mountain so tall,
I'm here dancing in that chaotic ball.
With laundry heaps begging for my attention,
I spin around, thwarting all apprehension.

In a world of whirlwinds, I try my best,
To laugh at the mess, and not feel stressed.
With each little stumble, I give a grin,
In this comical dance, I'm sure to win!

**When the World Unravels**

Alarm clocks sing, but I hit snooze,
Drinking cold coffee, what did I choose?
The dog wants a walk, I want to hide,
Navigating the chaos with my coffee guide.

The laundry's a tower, threatening a fall,
Ducks in a row? More like a brawl!
Slipping on toys, I play hopscotch with fate,
Juggling my breakfast, it's really first-rate!

The news is a whirlwind, oh what a scene,
Finding calm in the storm, like a meme.
A hiccup, a laugh, we roll with the tide,
In this wild adventure, let joy be our guide.

So when the day spins wildly around,
I'll capture the chaos, and wear it like a crown.
With a wink and a smile, I keep the light,
Turning everyday madness into sheer delight!

## A Symphony of Daily Struggles

Keys in the fridge and bread in the car,
Life plays a tune that's totally bizarre.
Chasing my coffee like a caffeinated hare,
Singing with toddlers, when I have the spare!

Pots are boiling, burning, oh dear,
I'm conducting this chaos with a hint of cheer.
The vacuum's a monster, I must tame,
Whirling and swirling, it's part of the game.

Dishes are stacking like a high-rise dream,
Building a masterpiece—till it starts to scream!
With laughter as my melody, I'll strum along,
In this symphony of madness, I definitely belong.

As I skip through each note, I glide with grace,
With rhythm and rhyme, life is my chase.
In the concerto of chaos, I find my song,
With each little hiccup, I know I belong!

## Navigating Through the Maze

I'm out here lost, in a very big maze,
Searching for snacks in a dreamy haze.
The cat's plotting mischief, I can sense their plot,
Navigating moments, giving it all that I've got.

Every turn I take leads to another surprise,
Found a remote, forgot where the time flies.
Sticky notes whisper, 'Remember the cake,'
But all I can think of is a nice coffee break.

I dodge every corner with laughter and sass,
Watching my worries as they seem to pass.
With a skip and a laugh, I dance through the stress,
Claiming my joy in this whimsical mess.

So here in my maze, I'll spin and I'll twirl,
Embracing the quirky and giving it a whirl.
With a chuckle, a grin, I'll refuse to be tame,
In this funny old maze, I'm loving the game!

## **Shadows in the Sunshine**

Chasing shadows in a sunbeam,
Dodging worries like a dream.
Laughter spills where chaos reigns,
Juggling thoughts like runaway trains.

Cup of coffee, slight misstep,
Coffee grounds on my plastic prep.
Balancing bills on a wobbly chair,
Hoping that fortune is feeling fair.

Socks mismatched, yet spirits high,
Lost a pen, watched it fly.
Each mishap is just comic gold,
Living stories that never get old.

So here we laugh, we fumble and roll,
In this maze, we play our role.
With every stumble, we dance and trip,
Navigating the wacky, let's take a dip.

## The Path of Patchwork

Bits of fabric, life's grand quilt,
Stitching moments, some are spilt.
Snags and patches tell our tale,
In mismatched colors, we prevail.

Kites that tangle in a breeze,
Socks that vanish, if you please!
Every thread, a slip or sway,
We patch them up, we're on our way.

Dinner burnt, the dog steals a bone,
An empty fridge, yet no one's alone.
Falling owls and rising dreams,
We laugh aloud, or so it seems.

Through the chaos, we proudly trod,
No map in sight, just a nod.
With our patchwork hearts, strong and true,
We weave a world, colorful too!

## **Threads of Connection**

Tangled wires and buzzing phones,
Strange connections, laughter groans.
Misplaced keys and lost goodbyes,
Yet we connect through goofy tries.

Texting typos, dinner fails,
Collecting stories, spinning tales.
Each missed call, a new delight,
We giggle through the endless night.

Puzzle pieces, none fit right,
Mismatched socks just feel so tight.
But in the mess, we find our way,
With laughter guiding every day.

So here we are, a motley crew,
Embracing oddities, that's our cue.
We may not follow a perfect script,
But joy, you see, is tightly whipped!

## Embracing the Shatter

This cup of coffee, shattered wide,
A splash of brown, it's not my pride.
Each drip laughs, spills on the floor,
A raucous cheer, 'Just one more!'

Life's a puzzle, pieces lost,
More like spaghetti, less like frost.
With every slip, I make a pact,
To find the humor in the fact.

Each broken plate tells a joke,
A clumsy dance, a funny poke.
When all seems wrong, I find the fun,
In every shatter, together we run.

So here's to cracks and every flaw,
Raise your glass, let's break the law.
In broken moments, laughter sings,
We catch our joy, as chaos clings.

## The Juggle of Jots

Notes are flying everywhere,
Post-its stuck to my cat's tail.
Coffee spills like sweet despair,
In my skills, I often fail.

Chasing tasks like wild balloons,
What was first is now a blur.
Lost in thoughts, I hum my tunes,
But the rhythm's such a stir.

Juggling dreams like circus stars,
Clumsy hands, a fumbling act.
Trying hard to mend the scars,
With a laugh, I stay intact.

Every day's a brand new chance,
To trip and fall, then rise again.
I may not have the best of plans,
But I'll conquer with a grin!

**Reverberations of Resolve**

Waking up to blaring alarms,
My trusty snooze is my best friend.
Pajamas worn like battle charms,
Defeat feels like it has no end.

Juggling issues, round and round,
With humor, I avoid the tumble.
Life's a theme park, joy profound,
But there's always room to grumble.

Flying papers, scattered dreams,
Like confetti in the air.
Who knew chaos could be schemes,
To bring laughter everywhere?

In this circus, I stand tall,
With a pie, I might slip and slide.
But I'll just laugh and mock the fall,
Through this ride, I'll take it in stride.

## Frayed Edges of Time

Time's a patchwork quilt I hold,
Stitches frayed, it's quite a sight.
Moments tangled, bright and bold,
Yet somehow, it feels just right.

Days that shuffle like a dance,
Twisted socks and missing keys.
Still I find a way to prance,
With every laugh, I feel at ease.

Calendar's a puzzle gone wild,
Colors clash like summer rain.
In this madness, I'm a child,
Spinning webs from purest pain.

And when I think I've lost the thread,
A chuckle brings the pieces near.
I'll stitch this chaos instead,
With joy, my vision stays quite clear.

## A Heartbeat in Chaos

In the whirlwind of the day,
My heart does a little jig.
Caffeine coursing like a play,
Fumbles felt, but oh so big.

Witty comebacks up my sleeve,
Where's my phone? What's the next aim?
Laughing so much, I can't believe,
Feels like a whimsical game.

Every mishap just adds flair,
Wobbling down this bumpy road.
Wit and charm are my hot air,
Lifting burdens, lightening load.

Breathless moments, joyful screams,
Chaos sings its funny tune.
I'll take this wild ride of dreams,
And dance 'neath the not-so-moon!

## Fragments of a Fraying Thread

Spilled coffee on my shirt, what a sight,
The cat has claimed my lap, it's their right.
Juggling tasks like clowns in a show,
Yet here I am, laughing at the blow.

Laundry's a mountain, dishes a sea,
I trip on my dreams and scrape my knee.
Plans laid with care, but they fly away,
Chasing after them feels like child's play.

Notes stuck on the fridge, a colorful spree,
Reminders of chores and forgotten tea.
With each tiny task, my to-do list grows,
Yet somehow I smile, despite all my woes.

Fragmented thoughts float like paper boats,
Each day a new game, see how it coats.
With a wink and a nudge, I embrace the absurd,
Our little circus, where laughter is heard.

## Balancing on a Tightrope

On a line stretched thin, I waddle and sway,
One wrong step, who knows? I might fly away!
With a coffee in hand and a shoe untied,
I dance with my fears, but don't let them hide.

The mail's overflowing, bills peek and grin,
Forget about diets, let the chaos begin!
Juggling my hopes like oranges, just right,
I'm a circus performer, my stage—daylight.

My balance is shaky, a comedy act,
Every mishap a punchline, a daily impact.
But if I can chuckle while teetering near,
Then perhaps this tightrope's not that severe.

Balloons full of dreams float above my head,
Dodging distractions like confetti instead.
One trip, one laugh, and I'm back on my feet,
In this big top show, I won't face defeat.

## The Art of the Daily Juggle

Morning sunshine bursts, a new act to try,
With toast in my hair, I wave breakfast goodbye.
Catch a stray sock, can you see it fly?
In this juggling act, the chaos grows spry.

Each task a ball, some bounce, some drop,
While spinning plates wobble, never do stop.
Chasing my thoughts, like ducks in a row,
But I laugh at the mess, it's my favorite show.

Emails and meetings, they dance in a line,
Yet somehow I twist, and it's all so divine.
Balancing wishes with plans not so clear,
The joy in the hustle keeps bringing me cheer.

As the day flips the script, I take a big bow,
In this hilarity, I promise to allow
The heart of the circus, my spirit, my pride,
In the art of the daily, I'll take it in stride.

## Between Chaos and Calm

The clock ticks loudly, a comedic beat,
My schedule's a puzzle, oh what a feat!
With mismatched socks and a coffee stain,
I'm tiptoeing through storms—what a rich refrain!

I sip on my chaos like it's fine wine,
With a wink at the mess, it all feels divine.
Laundry and laughter, dancin' hand in hand,
Truth is, I like this unruly, grand stand.

The calm's a mirage, behind it's a spree,
Of mishaps and giggles that cling to me.
I wear my resilience like a dazzling crown,
As I pirouette wildly, I never back down.

So here's to the moments, the scraps of delight,
Between calm and chaos, I'll dance through the night.
With humor my compass, I'll stroll this terrain,
Laughing my way past the joy and the strain.

## **Embracing the Uncertain**

Woke up today, tripped on a shoe,
Forgot my coffee, my brain's in a stew.
Spilled some cereal, it flew like a plane,
But hey, at least I can laugh at the strain.

Tax forms on my desk, a mountain to climb,
Counting my pennies, I'm out of my prime.
Netflix is calling, the couch is my throne,
I'll deal with tomorrow, today I'll postpone.

The cat's on the keyboard, typing away,
I think it's her way to say, "just play."
Worries can wait, the sun's shining bright,
I'll embrace the chaos, it feels kinda right.

So here's to the journey, the twists and the bends,
We're all just explorers, let's make some amends.
Laugh through the troubles, dance through the stress,
In this wobbly ride, we're all friends at best.

## Tattered Pages of Existence

Flip through my journal, oh what a sight,
A collection of mishaps, some wrongs and some right.
Coffee stains mingle with thoughts of despair,
Yet somehow there's humor lurking in there.

Forgotten groceries haunt my backseat,
An avocado, now ripe, smells bitterly sweet.
List of reminders, but where did it go?
Maybe my brain's been on cruise control slow.

Emails are piling, they dance in a queue,
'Urgent!' they shout, but I've lost my view.
Mundane concerns can take a back row,
With laughter as fuel, my worries will go.

So here's to the chapters, both wild and absurd,
To pen down our tales in a world that's disturbed.
Let's flip through these pages, with a grin on our face,
Tattered, but treasured, that's life's funny space.

**Anchored in the Now**

Sipping my drink, I think life is a jest,
The way it surprises, it's quite the guest.
Cats chase their tails, no trophy in sight,
But their silly antics bring pure delight.

Out the window, my neighbor does dance,
In his pajamas, he's taking a chance.
The dog gives a bark, as if to declare,
That joy is the treasure we all can share.

Juggling my plans, trying hard not to drop,
Checklists and timelines, oh, they make me stop.
But a chuckle breaks out, like sunshine so bright,
In the clutter of now, there's pure delight.

So here's to the moments, the giggles we find,
In the circus of life, let's not fall behind.
We'll savor the present, let worries defer,
In this grand mix-up, let's happily stir.

## The Dance of Dilemmas

Two roads diverged, and I chose the snacks,
To think of the choices now gives me some facts.
Should I take the stairs, or just stay on the ride?
My heart says to leap, but my feet want to hide.

A date on the calendar sparks some dread,
What kind of outfit? Where shall we tread?
I swirl in my closet, a fashion parade,
Yet nothing fits right, what choices I've made!

My phone's buzzing loud with reminders galore,
'Buy milk,' 'pay the bills,' 'don't forget the door!'
But amidst all the chaos, I do a quick spin,
Life's playful tango, I'm learning to win.

So let's twirl with the toss-ups, the twists and the turns,
For every misstep, a new lesson returns.
In this dance of dilemmas, I'll leap with delight,
With laughter as my partner, I'll glide through the night.

## **Patchwork of Hopes**

Sew a button on my dreams,
Stitching seams of silly schemes.
Tangled threads that never blend,
Knotting wishes round the bend.

Coffee spills and laundry piles,
Juggling chaos with a smile.
Every sock has found its mate,
Just ignore the odds and fate.

Lost my keys, it's quite the game,
Yet I stumble on the same.
Wishing walls would laugh and cheer,
At my antics year to year.

In this quilt of ups and downs,
With mismatched colors, silly clowns.
Hold my patchwork, all askew,
And let's laugh at what we do.

## **Whispering Troubles**

My to-do's trip on my feet,
Chasing giggles, missing beat.
Whispers float in friend's corral,
Troubles sigh and share a pal.

Laundry monsters hide away,
Playing peekaboo each day.
Dishes dance in sink's embrace,
Sing a tune of wild disgrace.

Neighbors prance in fuzzy socks,
Their loud antics twist and box.
Each complaint a jester's jest,
As we tumble in our quest.

With a wink, I chase the breeze,
Try to laugh with utmost ease.
In this circus, I take charge,
Stirring troubles, feeling large.

## **Surviving the Tides**

Waves crash down, I lose my hat,
Underwater flips and splat!
In this ocean of late bills,
I find treasures, quirky thrills.

Sailing boats made from my mind,
Where the wind is rarely kind.
Yet I paddle with great glee,
As the sea laughs back at me.

Riding high on foam and fun,
Sunshine gives a warming run.
With every splash, I break my fate,
Cracking jokes I can relate.

Swirling chaos in the sea,
Every wave a dance with me.
But I swim on, don't you fret,
In the tide, I feel no debt.

## In Search of Steady Ground

Tiptoeing on a wobbly line,
Searching for that place divine.
Every step a little jig,
Mimicking a dancing pig.

Voices echo in my head,
"Keep it cool!"—what's that they said?
As I trip on my own shoelace,
With a grin and wild embrace.

Finding balance in the mess,
Trying hard not to distress.
Yet I laugh at my own games,
As I fumble with outlandish claims.

In this hunt for solid base,
I discover purest grace.
Life's a circus, that's the sound,
Join the laughter all around.

## Weaving through the Uncertainties

Tangled threads in the grand design,
I laugh as I try to align.
With every stitch, a hopeful plea,
What a tangled mess still waits for me!

Spinning tales with each passing day,
Between the wrinkles, I find my way.
The fabric may fray, but I'll sew,
With a smile that helps my heart grow!

Yarns of jitter and floating fears,
I weave them tightly with witty sneers.
The patterns shift and sometimes clash,
But watch me twirl, it's a fun bash!

Amid the chaos, a stitch pops free,
I chuckle loud, for who could foresee?
This patchwork quilt of joy and strife,
Is just my way to embrace this life!

## In Search of the Missing Pieces

Puzzle pieces, scattered wide,
Like socks lost on a fun ride.
I lift the couch and check each nook,
Can I find them? Let's take a look!

Each piece I find brings such delight,
But wait—this corner just isn't right!
One piece is blue, the other's red,
I scratch my chin, "What's in my head?"

The cat steals one and runs away,
Chasing tails in a playful ballet.
I gather more as I start to think,
Each quirky part makes me smile and wink!

So here I sit, a crafty mess,
Finding joy in the game, I confess.
With laughter, I fit them side by side,
In this whimsical quest, I take great pride!

## The Silent Struggle of the Heart

My heart does cartwheels, all on its own,
Balancing feelings like a juggler's throne.
It whispers sweet nothings to empty air,
While I'm busy crawling through daily despair.

It twirls with laughter, then falls with sighs,
A comic routine, full of surprise.
I catch it grinning from ear to ear,
But when faces frown, it disappears!

In the circus of feelings, I play the part,
As clowns chase each other, I chase my heart.
With ups and downs in this funny dance,
Oh, to find love in a fleeting glance!

Yet still, I chuckle at the grand charade,
With missteps and bloopers, I won't be dismayed.
For even in struggles, I'll smile and play,
In this silent struggle, I'll find my way!

# Echoes from the Edge of Reason

I toe the line of sanity's brink,
With thoughts that change before I can think.
Muffled giggles in a crowded brain,
Teetering on edges, feeling a tad insane.

Conversations start, then ramble away,
Dear coffee cup, please help me stay.
One sip leads to a skip in the beat,
As logic giggles, I shuffle my feet.

Ideas bounce like a rubber ball,
Some soar high, while others crawl.
"Is this great wisdom?" I ponder aloud,
While my musings gather an imaginary crowd.

So here I stand on this cloud of thoughts,
Mixing the funny with what I've sought.
In echoes of laughter, I'll find my song,
Just dancing around where I feel I belong!

## **Resilience in the Face of Chaos**

I spilled my drink upon the floor,
The dog's now surfing through the door.
My sock's a hostage to the dryer,
But laughter lifts me ever higher.

The cat's in chaos, trees a-fall,
I wear mismatched shoes, but stand tall.
The world's a circus, I'm the clown,
Yet I manage to never frown.

My breakfast burnt, the clock's too fast,
I wave goodbye to sanity's cast.
With coffee spills and playful pets,
I find my joy, no regrets.

Through storms of socks and kitchen mess,
I dance around with pure finesse.
Embrace the wobbly, quirky ride,
For chaos is where dreams collide.

## A Patchwork of Days

My morning starts with cereal fuzz,
I cheer myself: 'It's all because!'
The cat left pawprints on my bread,
But I am still well-fed instead.

My schedule's soup, a twist and turn,
With noodles cooking, watch them churn.
I juggle tasks like circus acts,
In this patchwork quilt, I've got my facts.

The laundry screams for some respect,
While sock puppets demand neglect.
But hey, I dance between the piles,
As laughter bubbles up in smiles.

Each patch a memory, quilted tight,
With stitches of joy and tales of fright.
Though mismatched threads may show and fray,
I wear my chaos like a cabaret.

## **Whispered Hopes in the Storm**

Naps are fleeting, dreams are shy,
As thunder rumbles in the sky.
I sip my tea with trembling hands,
While counting life's odd, funny strands.

The dog howls low, the storm's got flair,
I find my peace in disarrayed hair.
With whispered hopes beneath the din,
I rise above each gusty spin.

I wear my jeans like battle scars,
With mismatched socks and hopes like stars.
A paper boat to brave the flood,
I float along in laughter's bud.

Through storms of laundry and playful noise,
I cherish chaos, it's my poise.
With every raindrop, I'll implore,
For happy whispers, I'll explore.

## The Art of Staying Afloat

I paddle through a sea of snack,
With wave of dishes at my back.
The dog's a lifeguard on the floor,
While I'm just trying to find the store.

An ocean of emails, surf's up high,
I ride the tide, but oh, I cry.
My boat's a mess, but that's okay,
I laugh at chaos in disarray.

With rubber ducks and spilt confetti,
I scale the cliffs of cluttered spaghetti.
A buoy of giggles keeps me true,
As tidal waves of work ensue.

So here I float on whimsy's tide,
In whirlpools of joy, I gently glide.
Embracing the waves, I'll never quit,
For laughter's the anchor in all of it.

## Equilibrium in Unease

I woke up today, what a surprise,
My socks don't match, what a great disguise.
Coffee spills down, suit looks a wreck,
Yet here I am, still on deck.

The cat's on my keyboard, typing away,
While bills pile high, they just want to play.
I juggle the chaos, a circus clown,
With a smile so bright, I won't let it down.

The clock's ticking loudly, it's time to be fast,
But my toast decided it didn't want to last.
I chase after dreams that run like a cat,
In this comedy show, I'm wearing a hat.

So here's to the moments, both silly and strange,
With ups and downs, it's all in the range.
Through giggles and stumbles, I'm making my way,
In this wacky dance, come what may.

## Moments Between Mayhem

At the break of dawn, my hair's a wild beast,
I'll take some toast, but I'll settle for least.
The dog has a secret, he's chewing my shoe,
While the clock mocks me, what am I to do?

I tripped on my laces, fell flat on my face,
Oh, what a morning, what a life race!
With laundry in ruins, I wear last week's flair,
These moments of mayhem, I choose to declare.

Breathe in, breathe out, a mantra I'll hum,
As the car starts to sputter, oh here it comes!
The traffic is thick, like molasses on toast,
But I'll laugh at the journey, it's the most I can boast.

So, here's to the wreck that we often call bright,
In the mayhem of living, we can find our delight.
With each twist and turn, I'm learning to play,
Embracing the chaos, come what may.

## **Holding on by a Thread**

My schedule's a puzzle, pieces just miss,
With meetings and deadlines, it feels like a quiz.
My coffee won the battle, it's winning again,
As I juggle my worries and my favorite pen.

The kid's toast is burnt, and crumbs fill the floor,
And just when I think, there's one thing more!
The phone starts to buzz, it's a friend from the past,
"Lend me some sanity!" I'll call her, at last.

Balloons in my car, they float to the sky,
Like my scattered thoughts, I just let them fly.
I'm holding on tight, but it's such a thin thread,
In this circus of life, I refuse to dread.

So I'll wear my bright smile, through wins and the flops,
Find joy in the chaos, while the world hops.
With laughter as armor, I'll navigate this,
In the wild web of moments, I find my bliss.

## The Balance of Being

I woke up this morning in a whirlwind spin,
With laundry gone rogue and dishes a din.
I dance through the clutter, it's part of my groove,
In this balance of chaos, I start to move.

My plants are still living, miraculously green,
While my vacuum has vanished, where could it be seen?
Life's like a seesaw, teetering high,
Yet I'm laughing aloud, as the days scurry by.

Through hiccups and giggles, I try to embrace,
The thrills and the tumbles, the wild, crazy race.
Every wobble and wobble, each stumble, each jest,
In the balance of being, I find what is best.

So let's toast to the moments, both silly and grand,
As we juggle our lives, on this bumpy road's strand.
With a wink and a chuckle, I carry my load,
In this balance of being, let's hit the road.

## Escaping the Squeeze

Woke up today, head in a spin,
Coffee's my buddy, let the circus begin!
Juggling my socks and a sandwich too,
I laugh at the chaos, what else can I do?

My inbox is full, like a clown car of dread,
Each email a pie, pie in my head!
Balancing deadlines, it's a whole new art,
With a smile on my face and a slight racing heart.

Dancing on deadlines, I twirl and I sway,
At the end of the tunnel, there's always a way.
Bumping into walls, yet still, I shall glide,
So bring on the chaos, I'll flip it with pride!

So chasing the sun, in my mismatched shoes,
Each step feels like one big headline news.
With laughter my armor, I'm ready to face,
This whirlwind of life — what a wild race!

# Dance of the Disrupted

My morning breakdance to the coffee machine,
One toe in my shoe, I'm a bit unsure, keen.
The toast does a flip, the cat takes a leap,
Together we chuckle, let's not skip a beat!

Outsourcing my fumbles to cartoonish flair,
I trip on the rug, but find magic in air.
With socks that don't match and hair wild like fire,
I sway like a dancer, with never a tire.

A tumble, a laugh, my sanity's thread,
I twirl through the mess, hearing life's misread.
Balances are fleeting, but action's a must,
Exceptional chaos in silliness' trust.

Here's to the glitches, the ups and the downs,
I'll wear this goofy smile, discard my frowns.
With rhythmic missteps, I'll waltz through this spree,
Finding joy in the furrows that dance just for me.

## Solace in Fragility

In moments of chaos, I sip on my tea,
A cup of sweet solace, just waiting for me.
The world's flipping pages, it's hard to keep track,
But laughter's a remedy; I'm glad for the crack.

The dishes are stacked, like a tower of dreams,
Fall apart with a clatter, or so it seems.
Yet each shattered piece holds a glint of delight,
In this fragile ballet, I'll dance through the night.

With whimsies and wonders, let's take on the wave,
A mud pie is art, and I'll learn how to brave.
Life's quirks may surprise, but I'll wear them with grace,
A jester's heart blooming, in this whimsical place.

So when the storm rattles, I toss my big grin,
Embrace all the mess, that is where I begin.
Fragile yet daring, through giggles I roam,
In the hilarity's grip, I carve out my home.

## The Palette of Perseverance

Brushstrokes of chaos on a canvas so wide,
Mixing colors of mayhem, oh what a ride!
Each drop a reminder that things fall apart,
Yet vibrant and zany, it's a true work of art.

With splatters of laughter, I paint on a wall,
And giggles are colors that run down it all.
The kitchen's a studio, the cat's in the scene,
A masterpiece forming in this joyful routine.

A pinch of disaster, a splash of delight,
My palette may tremble, but I grip it tight.
With every new stroke, I embrace the unknown,
For perseverance shines where the seeds of joy've grown.

So let's celebrate blunders, the colors that clash,
In this whimsical gallery, I cherish each splash.
With brush in my hand and a wink to the sky,
The art of existence — oh my, oh my!

## Threading the Needle of Existence

Woke up today, coffee spills,
My plans are like those spinning wheels.
Socks don't match, who needs the pairs?
Life's like circus, full of snares.

Juggling tasks, I grab my phone,
Still can't find that missing bone.
Chasing clocks, they run away,
My to-do list just loves to play.

Thought I'd bake, smoke filled the air,
The smoke alarm sings, it's quite unfair.
Burnt my toast, threw in some jam,
Guess it's dinner with a side of Spam.

But through the chaos, laughter rings,
Despite the mess, joy still clings.
Each day a rodeo, they can't unseat,
Time for a dance, on my own two feet.

## Tangled Threads of Tomorrow

My thoughts are knots, a tangled skein,
The more I try, the more I feign.
Dreams intertwine, like yarn in a ball,
Just want to kick back, and have a ball.

Tangled messages on my phone,
Who wants to talk? I'd rather moan!
Texting my friend, 'Where you at?'
Seems that she's stuck with her cat.

Future plans are in a twist,
Hoping it won't turn to mist.
Yet giggles emerge from tangled threads,
Delicious chaos feeds my feds.

Still, I sip tea through all this mess,
Absurdity's my daily dress.
As I unravel woes with glee,
Tomorrow's just as wild, you see!

## **Balancing Act on a Tightrope**

Walking on this wobbly line,
Got my balance? Well, it's fine!
Coffee in one hand, phone in the other,
Trying not to drop each task like a mother.

A cat runs by, it clips my toe,
Whoa there, buddy, just take it slow!
Balancing bills with giggles and food,
Who knew adulthood's such a shrewd mood?

Life's a circus, hold on tight,
Laughing while I face my plight.
High above a sea of dread,
Do I fly or fall? I'll just tread.

Yet if I trip, I'll just make a show,
A pratfall here, a wink, and let's go!
Every slip is just part of the game,
As I juggle this chaos, I'm never the same.

## Juggling the Pieces of Me

Got my hats, got my masks,
Juggling all these silly tasks.
A chef, a friend, a clown—oh me!
Trying to be the best I can be.

One minute I'm serious, next I'm a fool,
Balancing thoughts like a juggling school.
My cat in my arms, takes a mighty leap,
Now I'm just a mess, can't get past the heap.

Every day's a circus, every moment's a trip,
Dropping my dreams while I take a sip.
But as I laugh and toss them high,
I find joy in the crazy why.

The pieces may scatter, land just so,
But laughter's the glue, don't you know?
Through all this juggling, I'll find my way,
With a chuckle or two, we'll seize the day!

## **A Symphony of Strain**

I'm juggling fruit, a cat on my head,
My coffee is cold, and I'm still in bed.
The toast is on fire, the phone's ringing loud,
I wave to my neighbors, feeling quite proud.

I tripped on a sock, now the dog takes a run,
The plants need some water, I'm not sure it's fun.
The laundry's a mountain, the dishes, a flood,
But I wear my smile, and just laugh through the mud.

A circus of daily, absurdity's charm,
With spaghetti on walls, it's a familial warm.
I'll dance in the chaos, embrace the dismay,
In the uproar of life, I'm just here for the play.

With giggles and fumbles, I won't let it show,
That everything's madness, a wild, cosmic show.
From tantrums to tickles, all mixed in a blend,
This symphony's playing, on that I depend.

## Wading Through Whispers

In the quiet of corners, I fumble and fall,
Hearing echoes and murmurs, but it's just the wall.
I wear mismatched socks; they add to my flair,
And trip on the carpet, while no one's aware.

The whispers are giggles from friends in the hall,
As I dress like a clown, feeling ten feet tall.
Spilling my coffee right onto my shirt,
And laughing it off, 'cause hey, life's a flirt!

I've got sticky notes stuck all over my head,
Reminders of things, I was meant to have said.
I juggle my thoughts like they're balls made of air,
And wade through suggestions with "Who put them there?"

Yet here I keep plodding, through whispers and sneezes,
Where chaos is comfy, and laughter just pleases.
With each tiny slip, I'm just finding a way,
To dance through the madness, and enjoy the play.

## A Canvas of Contrasts

I paint with my breakfast, a splash of red jam,
On toast that's exploding, a real morning slam.
The sky's wearing gray, in a coat that's too tight,
While I'm running with kids in their miniature flight.

Life's hues are mixed up like crayons in drawers,
With laughter and tears spilling out through the doors.
I splatter some mustard on jeans that are blue,
While declaring the chaos a quirky debut.

But isn't it funny, this colorful ride?
Where prizes are found in the mess we can't hide.
From doodles to doodads, each moment demands,
That we relish the stirrings of life's clumsy hands.

So here's to the canvas, both messy and bright,
As I twirl through the colors like day turns to night.
With paints that are silly, and laughter at bay,
I'm crafting a picture that spins in dismay.

## Seeking Serenity in Spills

In my quest for a calm, I pour tea with flair,
But the kettle's too loud, I forget it's there.
I'm tangled in thoughts, like a yarn-bombed street,
Trying to find balance on unsteady feet.

The cake that I baked is an epic fail,
With frosting like glue and a smell akin to hail.
I laugh with my friends, as they dive for a bite,
Complaining aloud, "It's creative tonight!"

My zen is a puzzle, with edges that warp,
While the cat starts a fight with the neighbor's porch tarp.

We blend noisy moments with silence so sweet,
In the chaos we mingle, it's all a grand feat.

So here's to the spills that make the sun shine bright,
To the moments that sparkle, in the wildest of night.
For seeking that calm, let's sip on a cheer,
And embrace every hiccup that brings us all near.

## From Ashes to Ascendance

I dropped my toast, it hit the floor,
A sign of fate, I can't ignore.
The coffee spills, oh what a sight,
But laughter dances in the light.

My plants are wilting, what a tease,
They thrive on sunlight, not my sneeze.
Yet every glance at their green eye,
Makes me believe that they won't die.

With socks that clash, I start the day,
My wardrobe's fighting, come what may.
A little chaos makes it fun,
Who knew adulthood weighed a ton?

Yet from the wreckage, I arise,
With mismatched shoes and hopeful eyes.
For in the mess, I find my spark,
A wild rose blooming in the dark.

## **Souls Adrift**

In a sea of laundry, lost I roam,
Searching for socks that feel like home.
The dishes pile like mountains high,
Yet here I stand, and still, I try.

A calendar's filled with blurry dates,
I juggle dreams, while life just waits.
I laugh at plans all tossed away,
A circus act of disarray.

My coffee's cold, the toast is burnt,
For breakfast bliss, I'm always turned.
But flipping pancakes brings me cheer,
With syrup rivers, hoot and leer.

The world may swirl, but guess what's neat?
This tangled tale is pretty sweet.
With every twist, I hear the hum,
That life's a dance, so here I come!

## Finding Footing on Shifting Sands

I step on sand that's still too hot,
And slip and tumble in the plot.
My flip-flops fly, my sun hat's gone,
But giggles echo as I yawn.

A piña colada spills like dreams,
While seagulls squawk and strange sunbeams.
I chase the shore, but it retreats,
Like plans I make with wobbly feats.

The waves crash loud, they sing my plight,
Yet I find joy in this wild fight.
Like surfboards dancing in the spray,
I may just learn to ride the play.

So here I stand and stretch my arms,
Embracing chaos and its charms.
For even in this sandy jest,
I find delight and endless zest.

## The Bridges We Build

With duct tape dreams and hammer's clinks,
I mend my heart and make some links.
The architect's a goofy friend,
Who tells me laughter has no end.

We build with hopes and coffee cups,
A fortress made of all our ups.
Each brick of joy, each laugh we share,
Creates a path through any snare.

A bridge of memories, wide and free,
With every step, it comforts me.
Though storm clouds roll, I'll dance around,
No problem's too big when joy's found.

Our structure wobbles, yet it stands,
With funny tales and hopeful hands.
So here's to bridges built with grace,
In every stumble, we find our place.

**The Melody of Milestones**

Each birthday sneaks up; where did the time go?
I swear just last week I was out stealing snow.
Piles of laundry dance like they're ready to cha-cha,
A sock left alone is a modern-day drama.

Mornings are wild like a zoo on parade,
Coffee's a sidekick, keeps me unafraid.
The kids have their antics, oh what a show,
I laugh through the chaos; it's one hell of a show.

Maps of my dreams, I can't find the way,
Plans filled with laughter seem lost in the fray.
But with every misstep, I trip and I roll,
Finding joy in the journey, that's my secret goal.

So here's to the moments, both chaos and cheer,
I'll dance like a fool, with nothing to fear.
With mishaps to spare and puns on my tongue,
Life's a raucous ballad, forever unsung.

## Unseen Shifts

Every time I blink, something changes fast,
Yesterday's worries now seem like a blast.
My plants know the secrets, they sway like they care,
While I'm still deciding just what's in my hair.

Cereal's a breakfast of champions, they say,
While I'm just thankful it's keeping the gremlins at bay.
The dog has my shoes; my cat's on the shelf,
I guess it's a thrum of a life lived quite well.

The clock spins around like it's trying to dance,
I'm here in the quiet, missing my chance.
But laughter is fuel; it keeps engines bright,
Turn up the volume, let's party all night!

With every small shift, I find a new cheer,
Like finding the cookie when I thought it was beer.
I'm chasing the sips of my time-bound delight,
So here's to the shifts hidden out of sight.

## The Strength in Surrender

Sometimes I bow down to the laundry's demands,
It towers like mountains, respects my commands.
I raise a white flag: "You win, my dear friend!"
Let the socks conquer, my sanity's end.

Trying to juggle, I drop every ball,
The cat's quite impressed; he's seeing my fall.
Plans go awry, like a kite in the breeze,
But laughter's the rule; I'll float with such ease.

I've learned to embrace that I'm just a hot mess,
With chaos and giggles, who could ever guess?
Sometimes I'll shout: "This is how I thrive!"
With a wink and a grin, I'm simply alive.

So let's raise a toast to the unexpected,
To moments that leave our sanity wrecked.
With giggles and sighs, my spirit won't tire,
In strength through surrender, I find my true fire.

## Violin Strings and Tattered Dreams

My dreams are like strings on a violin tight,
Some days they sing, and some days they fight.
The notes all get tangled, a cacophony played,
I laugh at my failures; they'll never invade.

Waking up late and forgetting the scores,
I slip on my shoes while my brain clocks the chores.
The universe chuckles when plans go amiss,
It's music I dance to, don't take it amiss.

Tattered and torn, but still sweet to behold,
Each string that gets plucked tells a story so bold.
With every misstep, I discover my song,
A symphony woven where I truly belong.

So here's to the chaos that sets us apart,
To the melody made from the strings of the heart.
In laughter and harmony, I'll make my stand,
With violins playing, I'll dance on this land.

## Mosaic of Moments

Coffee spills in my lap, oh dear,
I laugh it off, not shedding a tear.
The dog steals my sandwich with pride,
I chase him down, what a wild ride!

Bouncing checks like a rubber ball,
Hoping the neighbors don't see my fall.
Juggling tasks like a circus clown,
Some days I'm up, some days I'm down.

Puzzles scattered on the floor,
Looking for pieces, where's the score?
I trip over dreams left on the rug,
But still, I smile, give life a shrug.

Chaos reigns but I can't complain,
Each little mishap, a silly gain.
With laughter my armor, I press on,
In this quirky dance, I'm never gone.

## The Fragile Dance of Existence

Woke up today, socks don't match,
Found some ketchup, what a catch!
The toast is burnt but who can tell?
I'll just pretend all's going swell.

I pirouette past the laundry pile,
Balancing bills with a quirky smile.
Spinning plates like it's my fate,
Hoping they won't smash or wait!

Every phone call's a wild quiz,
Is this the time I just say, "Fizz"?
I answer with laughter, an artful reply,
Dancing through life, oh me, oh my!

With sticky notes plastered everywhere,
I chase my own thoughts, catch me if you dare!
In this wacky waltz, I find my groove,
Fumbling and fumbling, but still I move.

## **Holding Up the Weight of Dreams**

Carrying hopes like a bumpy ride,
A suitcase of laughter, a heart full of pride.
Tripping on wishes scattered around,
Each tiny stumble, a whimsical sound.

The map is scribbled, directions unclear,
Lost in my thoughts, but I'm still here.
With a wink to the universe, I beg and plead,
To guide my feet in this hilarious lead.

I bend like a tree in a comical breeze,
Dancing to rhythms that bring me to my knees.
I gather my thoughts like autumn leaves,
In this silly chaos, my spirit believes.

A backpack of dreams, I carry it tight,
With laughter my spark, I take on the night.
Falling and laughing, I make the best show,
In this odd, lovely journey, I grow and glow.

## Echoes of a Tattered Heart

My heart's a quilt of mismatched threads,
Each square a story, some fillers, some spreads.
Singing out tunes that are out of key,
Echoing laughter as I spill my tea.

In a world of chaos, I find my beat,
Stumbling on joy, a messy retreat.
Collecting my fragments, I tape, I glue,
Each patch a treasure, a laugh or two.

Bouncing off walls like a rubber ball,
Chasing my thoughts, lucky if I recall.
With every slip, I discover my art,
In this mad collage, beats my tattered heart.

In the echoes of giggles, I find my place,
A comedy show, with a smiley face.
Embracing the mess, I'll never depart,
In this whirlwind of moments, beats my heart.

## **Strength in Stumbling**

I tripped over my own two feet,
Laughter echoed in the street.
My coffee splashed, a messy feat,
Yet somehow, I found it sweet.

Falling down, I take a bow,
Time to laugh, I'll take a vow.
Tip over and then get up now,
Clumsiness is my know-how.

## Navigating the Near Misses

I dodged the bus by half a hair,
Said a prayer—didn't care.
Missed my stop, but what a scare,
Life's a circus, I'm the bear.

Stumbling past my shoelace ties,
Watching where my coffee flies.
Every slip, a new surprise,
Oh my, how the morning flies!

**Gentle Reminders**

Smiling as I walk the line,
Tripping while I sip my wine.
"Hey, watch out!" Oh, I'm just fine,
Each mishap's a fun design.

Post-it notes and frantic plans,
Where's my phone? Where's my pants?
Gentle nudges, silly dance,
Life's absurd—let's take a chance!

## Flickers of Fortitude

I juggle dreams and socks galore,
Forgotten keys and forgotten lore.
Beaming bright, though I'm a bore,
Who knew growing up means more?

Wobbling through the daily grind,
With oops and laughs, I'm so aligned.
Each little fail is redefined,
In all the chaos, joy is mined.

## **Threads of Silver in the Fabric of Time**

In the closet of chaos, we hide our shoes,
With mismatched socks, oh, what a ruse!
Time flies by like a caffeinated ant,
While we sip our coffee, wondering where it went.

The to-do list grows like a weed in spring,
With tasks that jiggle, jump, and cling.
We chase our tails, oh, what pure delight,
As everything jumbles into a comical sight.

We stitch our dreams with a needle of hope,
Yet trip on the stitches, learning to cope.
With laughter and bubbles, we take a dive,
In this fabric of time, we just strive to survive.

So let's embrace the mess, the joyful spree,
In the chaos of threads, we dance wild and free.
For every mishap is a tale to tell,
In the tapestry of life, we're doing quite well.

## The Balance Between Now and Tomorrow

A juggler's act in a three-ring fight,
Balancing now with the future so bright.
We spin our plates like a circus show,
While past mistakes beg, "Hey, don't let go!"

To plan or not to plan, that is the game,
As calendars laugh and call out our name.
We write the agenda that life just ignores,
And chase after moments like whimsical chores.

With coffee in hand and a list in our head,
We set out each day to earn our daily bread.
But watch out for squirrels, they'll distract you for sure,
And suddenly you're lost in a quest for the pure.

So here's to the balance we find every week,
Between dreams we pursue and the chaos we seek.
In this circus of now and tomorrows so bright,
We laugh at the juggle, it all feels just right.

## The Fragility of Holding On

With fingers like noodles, we grasp at the day,
Holding on to moments that slip right away.
Like trying to catch water with a handful of sand,
We fumble and bumble, just doing the best we can.

We try to control what twists like a vine,
But plans have their own mind, oh how they entwine!
As schedules unravel, we grin through the mess,
With a wink to the universe, it's all just a jest.

We cling to our hopes on a thread that's so thin,
Like a cat in a tree thinking, "How did I begin?"
But laughter erupts as we tumble and sway,
In the dance of the fragile, let's cherish today.

So here's to the chaos, the slips and the falls,
To the stories we weave in the midst of our brawls.
For in holding on tight, with some grace and some fun,
We find in that chaos, we all are as one.

# Fragments of a Shattered Dream

In pieces we gather our hopes and our schemes,
Like a jigsaw puzzle of fractured dreams.
We search for the corners, we hunt for the skies,
As each little fragment just humorously lies.

A plan was laid out like a map on the floor,
Then a burst of confetti! Now, where's that door?
As we pick up the shards with an optimistic cheer,
Each slip and each trip brings the laughter near.

With glue and with glitter, we craft what we can,
A masterpiece born from the heart of a fan.
It might not be perfect, but here's the surprise:
In the shards of our dreaming, a new hope will rise.

So toast to the broken, the silly and strange,
For in every mishap, there's magic to exchange.
With laughter our glue, and love our bright beam,
We create our own canvas from fragments of dream.

## Sculpting Shadows

Chasing my own feet, it's quite the game,
Trip over shoes, yet I feel no shame.
With each awkward step, I dance with my day,
Wobbling through life in a comical way.

Mirror reflects a face full of cheer,
Yet behind the mask, I'm filled with fear.
Sculpting my shadows, they laugh and they play,
Juggling my worries like bright colored clay.

Mismatched socks and a shirt full of stains,
Trying to adult amidst all these pains.
But laughter is key when I'm losing the fight,
So I'll stumble on boldly, from morning to night.

At the end of the day, with a wink and a grin,
I may not have won, but man, did I spin!
With each clumsy moment, I craft my own tale,
Sculpting my shadows; I'll never turn pale.

## Quiet Battles

In the kitchen, I wage a fierce war,
Against the microwave, open your door!
Popcorn explodes like it's refuse to tame,
While I quietly whisper, 'Who needs this game?'

Coffee spills out; oh, what a delight!
PJs and sweatpants, my armor each night.
Battles with toast, that refuses to brown,
Yet somehow I rise, in this glorious gown.

The clock's not my friend, it ticks way too slow,
Can't find my keys; where did they go?
A war zone of socks, and dishes to slay,
Yet laughter can conquer the chaos of day.

So here's to the battles, the small and the grand,
Waging them quietly, it's all part of the plan.
With a grin on my face and a heart full of cheer,
I'll march on ahead, 'cause tomorrow's right here.

## **The Colors of Chaos**

Crayons and markers spread all on the floor,
Painting my worries, oh, to be four!
With colors that bleed and sketchy lines,
I mix up my thoughts like they're expensive wines.

Each day's a canvas, splashed wild and bright,
Yet somehow it turns out a glorious sight.
With purpled skies and orange trees,
I laugh at the chaos; it's all a tease.

My plans may unravel at the slightest breeze,
But the colors of chaos bring me to ease.
Scribbles of joy on a foggy old page,
In this vibrant circus, I gladly engage.

So here's to the mess, it's the spice of the show,
I'll dance in the rain with a flamboyant glow.
With a splash and a dash, I paint my own way,
In the colors of chaos, I'll forever stay!

## In the Wake of Waves

Surfing through days with a quirky vibe,
Balancing my toast on a wobbly tribe.
Each morning's a swell, built up from the night,
Yet I hit the shore and I'm ready to bite.

The tide pulls away, but I'm tangled still,
Paddle out to sea with a coffee-filled thrill.
Dodging my worries like a pro on a board,
Finding the humor in every award.

An ocean of laughter crashes on rocks,
Floating through chaos, avoiding the socks.
The waves may be wild as they roll and they churn,
But I catch the laughter; it's my turn to learn.

So here's to the beach, where the fun never ends,
I ride all my troubles; they're just silly bends.
In the wake of waves, I will splash and I'll soar,
Surfing through giggles, forever explore.

## Lighthouses in Darkness

A sock with holes is on my feet,
But I still dance to a funky beat.
My coffee spills, my shirt's askew,
Yet here I am, just seeing it through.

The cat has stolen my sandwich treat,
While I juggle tasks like they're on repeat.
The vacuum's roaring, the dishes stack,
But I can't help but laugh at this chaotic act.

My phone's alerting, what did I miss?
Oh right, it's just my grocery list.
Yet in the chaos I find my way,
Collecting smiles, come what may.

Through dizzy spins and upside down,
I'm just a jester in a paper crown.
With every stumble, I rise and cheer,
Finding joy in every little sphere.

## Raindrops on a Paper Roof

A tiny puddle on the floor,
Looks like a lake, oh what a chore!
The roof is leaking, it's quite absurd,
I dance around like a cheerful bird.

The weather man said sunny skies,
Yet here I stand with rain-filled eyes.
My umbrella's broke, it's upside down,
But I'm still laughing, oh what a clown.

The kids come running, splashing around,
I hide my shoes, can't let them drown.
With every dribble and every slip,
We share the chaos—what a trip!

So here's to raindrops and paper roofs,
Turning leaks into joyful goofs.
Through puddles deep and skies so gray,
I'll keep my giggles, come what may.

## The Heat of Healing

Burnt my toast, oh what a smell,
In the kitchen, it's chaos—what a tale to tell!
The smoke alarm sings a screechy tune,
But I'm still humming, dancing like a loon.

Dropped my phone, it bounced like a ball,
While I hunt for those keys that just won't call.
But through the flops and little spills,
I craft a giggle with all my skills.

A spilled potion, a chocolate stain,
Each mishap drives me a little insane.
Yet amidst the chaos, I find my grace,
With laughter lifting me from the chase.

So bring on the mess, the heat, the fun,
With every foible, I've already won.
For healing happens in the silly wise,
Where every blunder brings joyful surprise.

## Whispers of Worry

The laundry's piled, it's mountain high,
While doubts dance around, oh me, oh my!
Got bills to pay and shoes to tie,
Yet I'll wear mismatched socks, oh why not try?

Tried to cook but set off a flame,
My dinner plans? What a funny game!
With every mishap, I spark a grin,
In this wild circus, I twirl and spin.

The clock ticks louder, time slips away,
Yet here I stand, ready to play.
With whispers of worry, I'll turn it 'round,
Finding humor in chaos that's all around.

So here's to the jests, the fears we share,
They make us human, in laughter, we dare.
With a wink and a smile, let's dance through the fray,
In every stumble, find joy today.

## Stars amid Shadows

In the night, I trip and fall,
But laugh it off, I stand up tall.
With every slip, I gain new grace,
Finding joy in the chaos of space.

Juggling tasks like circus clowns,
Dropping things while wearing frowns.
A dance with chaos, oh so bright,
Stars shine through the darkest night.

I wear mismatched socks with pride,
A badge of humor, my trusted guide.
Life's a jest, I play along,
Singing softly my silly song.

Falling leaves and playful breeze,
A mess of laughter, if you please.
In shadows where worries once grew,
I find a laugh; it sees me through.

## The Space Between the Storms

Raindrops fall, yet here I stand,
Umbrella upside down, not as planned.
I grin at puddles, sailing away,
In my tiny boat of a bad rainy day.

The thunder grumbles, I laugh back,
Dancing barefoot, embracing the flack.
The sun peeks through, a ray of fun,
A game of hide and seek has begun.

Stormy weather makes quite the show,
I'm the star with nowhere to go.
Between the gales, I catch my breath,
Turning mischief into sweet lev.

Then comes the calm, soft as a dream,
I sip hot cocoa, a cozy theme.
Between the storms, a wink in time,
Finding laughter, my favorite rhyme.

**Catching the Broken Pieces**

With mismatched socks and a crooked tie,
I gather lost thoughts as they drift by.
Coffee spills, the morning's a mess,
Yet chaos turns into pure happiness.

I dodge the dust bunnies with a grin,
Catch my breath while the laughter spins.
Each little fracture, a story to share,
Henpecked humor beneath the despair.

Cracks in my plans make room for fun,
Like eyebrows raised at the rising sun.
Searching for joy in chaos's grasp,
Snagging giggles, tight smiles to clasp.

With every stumble, I learn to fly,
A jester's heart, reaching for the sky.
Collecting pieces, a mosaic delight,
Painting a picture of laughter in light.

## The Phoenix of Persistence

I rise from ashes, a quirky bird,
Flapping about like you've never heard.
Mistakes and flops, my trusty mates,
In this silly tale, I celebrate.

With feathers askew, I strut my stuff,
Belly laughs, oh life can be tough.
Yet here I am, with a wink of fate,
Each fragile moment, I appreciate.

Burning bright with humor's spark,
I light the way through the dark.
Though storms may brew and tempests swell,
I chant my mantra: all is well.

So let me soar, both high and low,
With every setback, I'll steal the show.
A phoenix of persistence, full of cheer,
I twirl through the troubles, hold them near.

## Breath of a Thousand Melodies

I woke up today, coffee in hand,
Missing my keys - isn't that grand?
Spilled my cereal, oh what a mess,
Thinking of you, it's all just a guess.

Dreams of quiet and clean, pristine,
My cat took a nap on my favorite bean.
Life's little hiccups, a comical show,
We're all just a circus, playing the role.

Juggling tasks like a clown in the ring,
Dancing to chaos, it makes my heart sing.
With laughter and mishaps sprinkled around,
Each breath a melody, joy can be found.

So I take a moment, breathe in the mayhem,
Embrace every blunder, my shimmering gem.
For in every misstep, a story builds up,
Cheers to the chaos, I'm raising a cup.

# Capturing Fleeting Whispers

Trying to balance my chores and my dreams,
Like walking a tightrope, or so it seems.
The clock's ticking loudly, it mocks my one plan,
Just me and my worries, a one-woman band.

I tripped on my dog, and fell on my face,
But laughter erupted, it lightened the space.
What's a little tumble when there's joy to be spread?
A giggle erupts straight from my head!

Chasing the sunlight through puddles of grief,
Snagging the moments, a comic relief.
Imperfect delights dance in my sight,
I capture them all, even in flight.

So come join my chaos, let's share every sigh,
Spin tales of mishaps with laughter nearby.
In fleeting whispers, we'll find our own cheer,
And toast to the moments that keep us sincere.

## Jigsaw of Juggling Hearts

A puzzle of feelings, all pieces askew,
Finding the corners, but losing a shoe.
Each day a new challenge, I laugh at the fray,
Like trying to paint while it's raining all day.

Dishes are piling, I'm late for my call,
Yet here I am giggling at it all.
The garden's a jungle, where weeds meet my fate,
But I water my laughter, and watch it create.

Balancing wishes like circus acts bold,
Wrapped in my chaos, I break from the mold.
Flipping through pages of hopes and surprise,
Winking at troubles, I see through their lies.

So let's juggle these hearts, spin stories of grace,
Laughter's our compass, we're finding our place.
In this jigsaw of life, we'll color the dark,
With giggles and dreams, we ignite the spark.

## The Weight of Tomorrow

Carrying worries like bags on my back,
Each one a story, each story a crack.
I shuffle through moments, they pile high and wide,
Yet somehow I smile, with joy as my guide.

Procrastination's my friend, we share quite a laugh,
As I dive into Netflix, forget the math.
The laundry's alive, a beast in the room,
Yet I twirl through the chaos, inviting the bloom.

List-making guru, my pen's on the go,
But who needs a checklist for a surreal show?
All those tomorrow's—the weight, it feels strange,
I toss them like confetti, embrace every change.

So sit with me here, let's linger a while,
We'll dance with the burdens and laugh with the trials.
For the weight of tomorrow can't hold down our glee,
Together we'll flutter, wild and free.

www.ingramcontent.com/pod-product-compliance
Lightning Source LLC
Chambersburg PA
CBHW051644160426
43209CB00004B/780